WE WILL REMEMBER THEM
MUSIC FOR REMEMBRANCE

for mixed-voice choirs

Published by
Novello Publishing Limited
14-15 Berners Street,
London W1T 3LJ, UK.

Exclusive Distributors:
Music Sales Limited
Distribution Centre, Newmarket Road,
Bury St Edmunds, Suffolk IP33 3YB, UK.

Music Sales Corporation
180 Madison Avenue, 24th Floor,
New York NY 10016, USA.

Music Sales Pty Limited
Units 3-4, 17 Willfox Street, Condell Park
NSW 2200, Australia.

Order No. NOV294811
ISBN 978-1-78305-681-1

Printed in the EU.

www.musicsalesclassical.com

We Will Remember Them
Music for Remembrance

for mixed-voice choirs

NOVELLO

Contents

We Will Remember Them
Music for Remembrance

We Will Remember Them is a collection of some of the finest pieces of choral music on the theme of remembrance. The volume is suitable for church, cathedral, school, youth and community choirs. It contains music appropriate for Remembrance Sunday services, and beautiful pieces suitable for concerts, memorial and funeral services, and other acts of remembrance and reflection.

The book includes classic choral works such as Samuel Barber's *Agnus Dei*, Edgar Bainton's *And I saw a new heaven* and William Harris's *Bring us, O Lord God* alongside other works by well-loved composers including John Tavener (*Funeral Ikos* and *Exhortation and Kohima*), Richard Rodney Bennett (*A Good-Night*), Paul Mealor (*In My Dreams*) and Eric Whitacre (*Nox aurumque*).

New arrangements, such as David Hill's choral reworking of Edward Elgar's *Nimrod*, are included with other new works by some of the best contemporary composers: Graham Fitkin's *A Christmas Truce*, Tarik O'Regan's *We Remember Them*, and Jeremy Dale Roberts's *I heard a voice*.

Agnus Dei

Samuel Barber
(1910-1981)

2

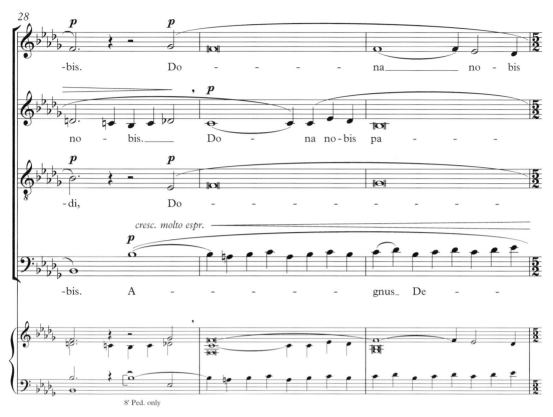

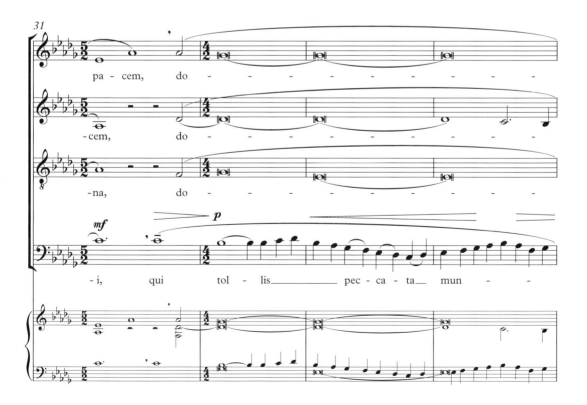

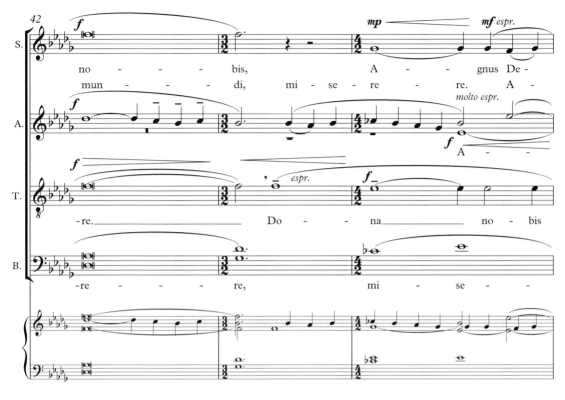

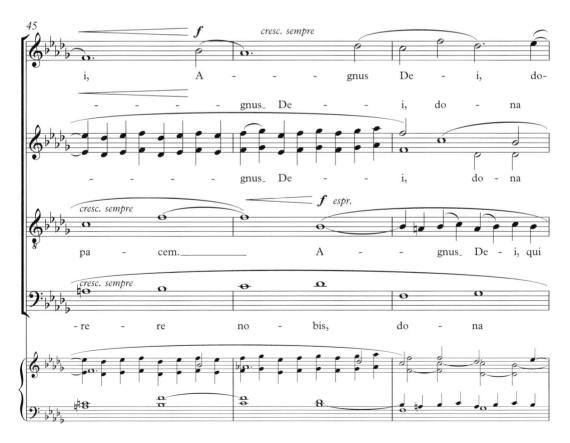

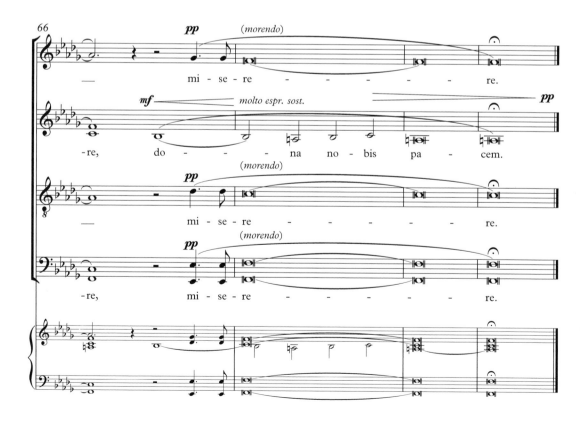

And I saw a new heaven

Revelation 21: 1-4

Edgar L. Bainton
(1880-1956)

14

bride a-dorn-ed for her hus - band.

bride a-dorn-ed for her hus - band.

-par - ed as a bride a-dorn-ed for her hus - band.

-par - ed as a bride a-dorn-ed for her hus - band.

And I heard a great voice out of heaven, say - ing,

18

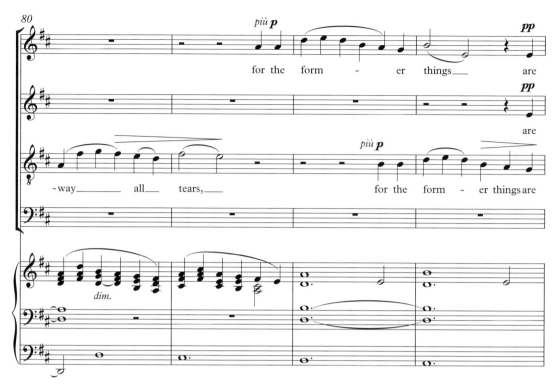

for the form - er things___ are
are
-way_____ all__ tears,_____ for the form - er things are

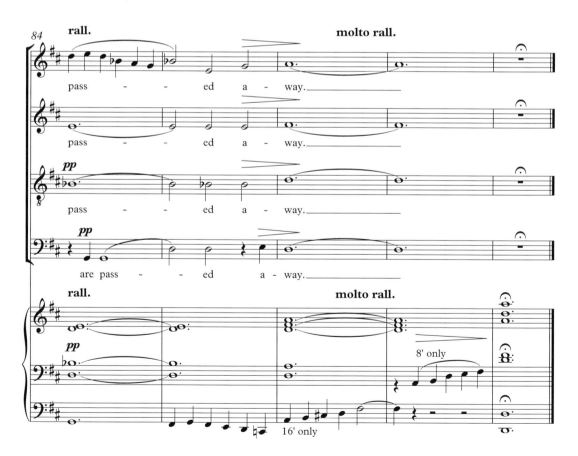

pass - - ed a - way._____
pass - - ed a - way._____
pass - - ed a - way._____
are pass - - ed a - way._____

Bring us, O Lord God

John Donne
(1572-1631)

William H. Harris
(1883-1973)

The Christmas Truce

Frederick Niven

Graham Fitkin
(b. 1963)

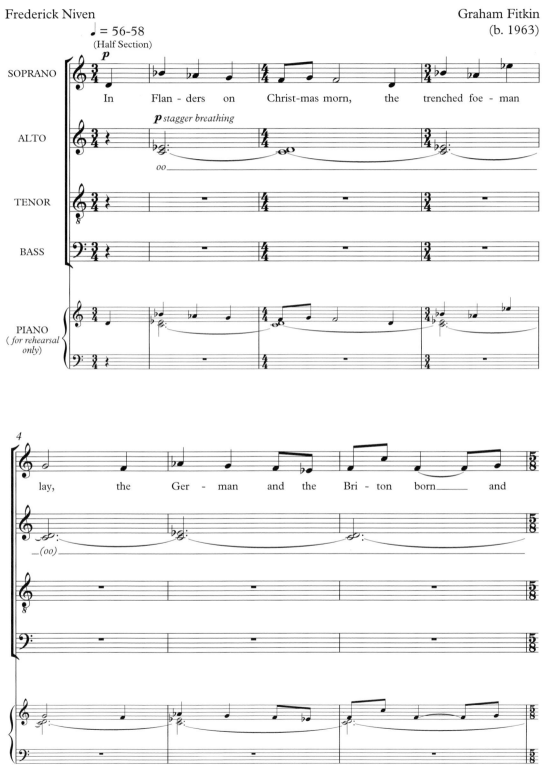

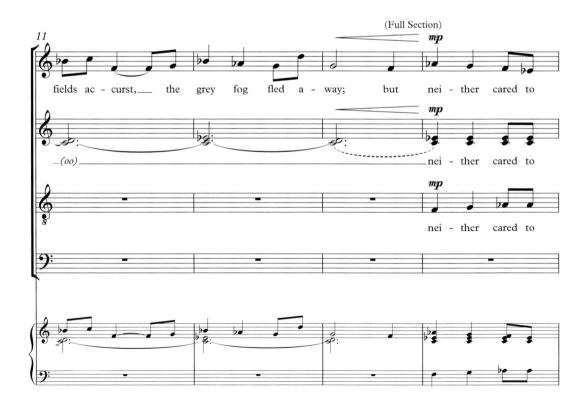

fire___ first, for it was Christ - mas Day.___

fire first, Christ - mas Day.___

fire first, Christ - mas Day.___ They

Day.___

A

ah___ oo___

ah___

called out from each to each, a - cross the dis - ar - ray, for dread - ful had

stagger breathing

ah___ oo___

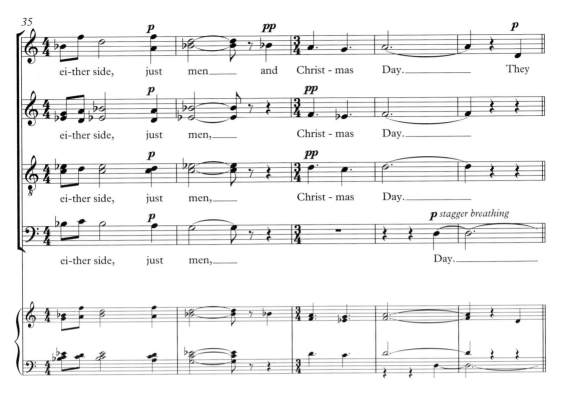

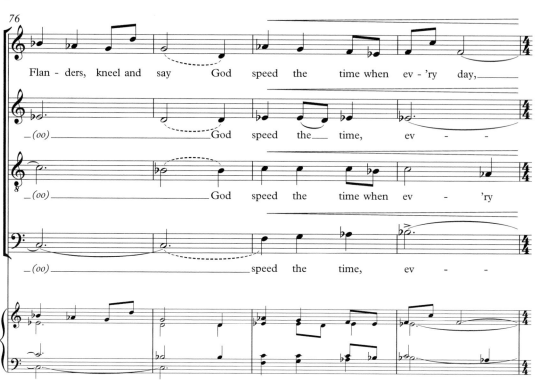

Exhortation and Kohima

1. The Exhortation

Laurence Binyon
(1869-1943)

John Tavener
(1944-2013)

50

2. Kohima

John Maxwell Edmonds
(1875-1958)

John Tavener
(1944-2013)

For your to - mor - row, we gave

our to - day.

in memory of E. T. C.

Funeral Ikos

from the Order for the
Burial of Dead Priests
trans. Isabel Hapgood (1851-1928)

John Tavener
(1944-2013)

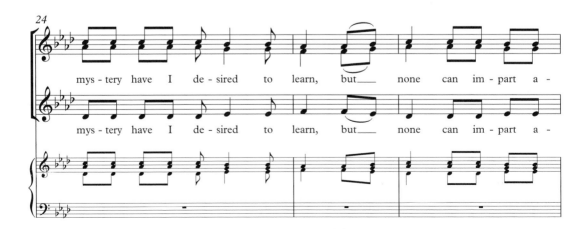

27

-right. Do they call to mind their own peo - ple, as we do them?_ Or

-right. Do they call to mind their own peo - ple, as we do them?_ Or

31

S. have they for - got - ten all those who mourn them and make the_ song: Al - le -

A. have they for - got - ten all those who mourn them and make the_ song: Al - le -

T. Al - le -

B. Al - le -

35

-lu - ia, Al - le - lu - ia, Al - le - lu - ia, Al - le - lu - ia.

-lu - ia, Al - le - lu - ia, Al - le - lu - ia, Al - le - lu - ia.

-lu - ia, Al - le - lu - ia, Al - le - lu - ia, Al - le - lu - ia.

-lu - ia, Al - le - lu - ia, Al - le - lu - ia, Al - le - lu - ia.

We go forth on the path e-ter-nal, and as con-demned, with down-cast fa-ces, pre-

-sent our-selves be-fore the on-ly God e-ter-nal. Where then is come-li-ness? Where

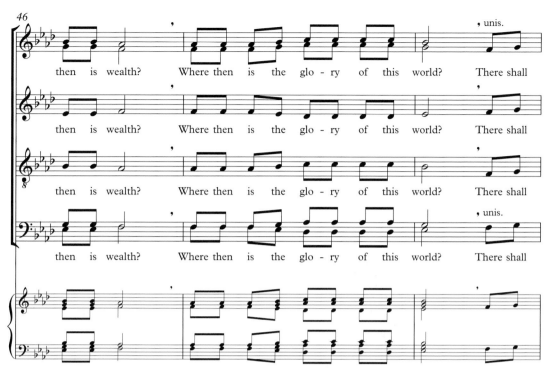

then is wealth? Where then is the glo-ry of this world? There shall

none of these things aid us, but on-ly to say__ oft the psalm:_ Al - le -

-lu - ia, Al - le - lu - ia, Al - le - lu - ia, Al - le - lu - ia.

-lu - ia, Al - le - lu - ia, Al - le - lu - ia, Al - le - lu - ia.

-lu - ia, Al - le - lu - ia, Al - le - lu - ia, Al - le - lu - ia.

-lu - ia, Al - le - lu - ia, Al - le - lu - ia, Al - le - lu - ia.

T.

B.

If thou hast shown mer - cy un - to man, O man, that same mer - cy shall be

If thou hast shown mer - cy un - to man, O man, that same mer - cy shall be

shown thee there; and if on an or - phan thou hast shown com - pas - sion, the same shall there de -

div.

shown thee there; and if on an or - phan thou hast shown com - pas - sion, the same shall there de -

Youth and the beau-ty of the bo-dy fade at the hour of death, and the tongue then

Youth and the beau-ty of the bo-dy fade at the hour of death, and the tongue then

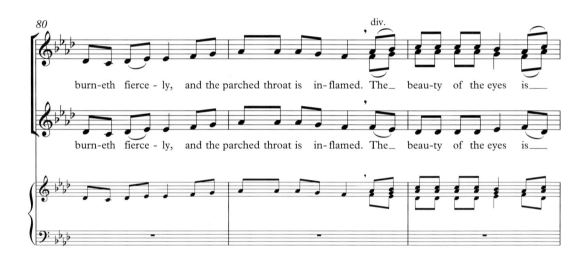

burn-eth fierce - ly, and the parched throat is in-flamed. The_ beau-ty of the eyes is___

burn-eth fierce - ly, and the parched throat is in-flamed. The_ beau-ty of the eyes is___

quenched then, the_ come-li-ness of the face all_ al - tered, the_ shape - li-ness of the

quenched then, the_ come-li-ness of the face all_ al - tered, the_ shape - li-ness of the

neck des-troyed; And the oth-er parts have be-come numb, nor of-ten__ say: Al-le-

neck des-troyed; And the oth-er parts have be-come numb, nor of-ten__ say: Al-le-

Al-le-

Al-le-

-lu-ia, Al-le-lu-ia, Al-le-lu-ia, Al-le-lu-ia.

-lu-ia, Al-le-lu-ia, Al-le-lu-ia, Al-le-lu-ia.

-lu-ia, Al-le-lu-ia, Al-le-lu-ia, Al-le-lu-ia.

-lu-ia, Al-le-lu-ia, Al-le-lu-ia, Al-le-lu-ia.

With_ ec-stas-y are we in-flamed if we but hear that there is light e-ter-nal yon-der; that

With_ ec-stas-y are we in-flamed if we but hear that there is light e-ter-nal yon-der; that

With_ ec-stas-y are we in-flamed if we but hear that there is light e-ter-nal yon-der; that

With_ ec-stas-y are we in-flamed if we but hear that there is light e-ter-nal yon-der; that

there is Pa-ra-dise, where-in eve-ry soul of Right-eous Ones re-joic-eth. Let us all,

there is Pa-ra-dise, where-in eve-ry soul of Right-eous Ones re-joic-eth. Let us all,

there is Pa-ra-dise, where-in eve-ry soul of Right-eous Ones re-joic-eth. Let us all,

there is Pa-ra-dise, where-in eve-ry soul of Right-eous Ones re-joic-eth. Let us all,

al - so, en - ter in - to Christ, that all we may cry a - loud thus un - to God:

Al - le - lu - ia, Al - le - lu - ia, Al - le - lu - ia, Al - le - lu - ia.

1981

God is our hope and strength

Psalm 46: 1-3, 5, 7-10

A. Herbert Brewer
(1865-1928)

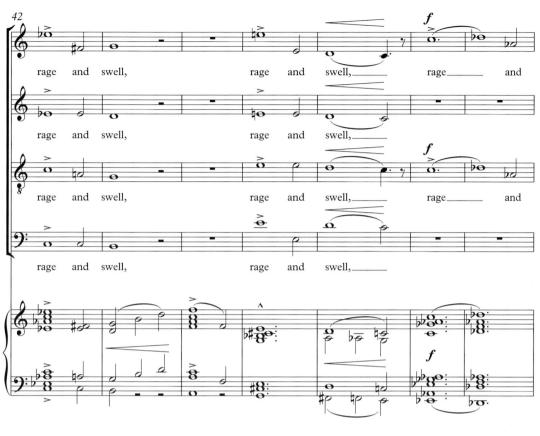

rage and swell, rage and swell, rage and

rage and swell, rage and swell,

rage and swell, rage and swell, rage and

rage and swell, rage and swell,

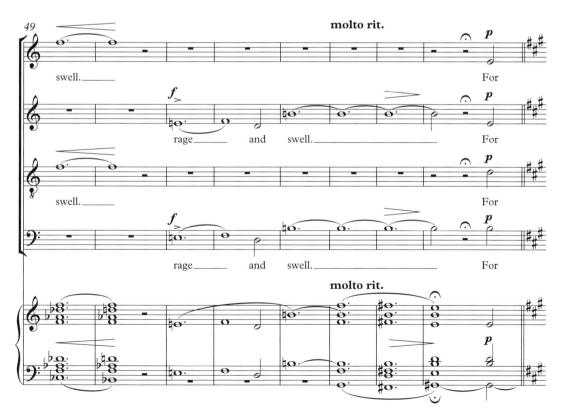

swell. For

rage and swell. For

swell. For

rage and swell. For

molto rit.

He is ex - alt - ed a-mong the hea-then, he is ex - alt - ed

He__ is ex - alt - ed in__

He is ex - alt-ed a - mong__ the

He is ex - alt-ed a - mong__ the hea -

in the earth, he is ex - alt - ed in the earth. God is in the

the earth. God is in the

hea - then. God is in the

- then.__ God is in the

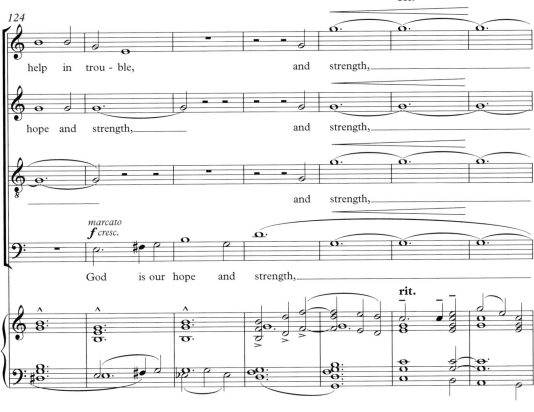

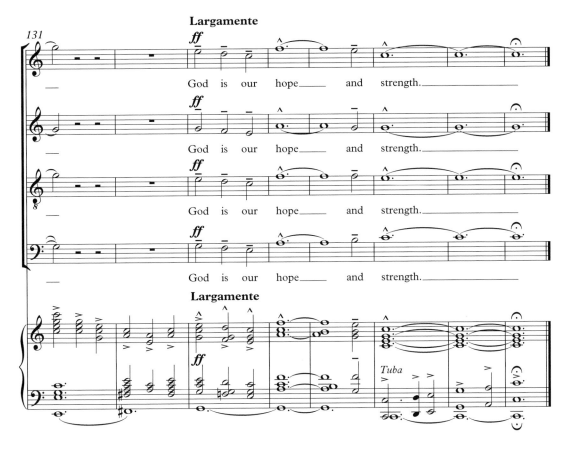

for Paul, in memory of Linda

A Good-Night

Francis Quarles
(1592–1644)

Richard Rodney Bennett
(1936-2012)

Holy is the true light

Salisbury Diurnal
trans. G. H. Palmer (1842-1933)

Ernest Bullock
(1890-1979)

For the Fallen

Laurence Binyon
(1869-1943)

David Terry
(b. 1975)

They shall grow not old, as we that are left grow old:

Age shall not wea - ry them, nor the years con - demn. At the

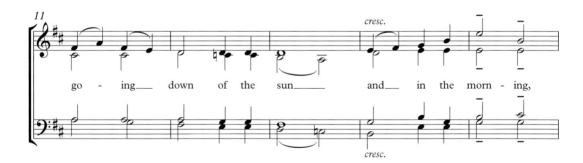

go - ing down of the sun and in the morn - ing,

We will re - mem - ber them, we will re - mem - ber them.

5 November 2013

Holy is the true light

Salisbury Diurnal
trans. G. H. Palmer (1842-1933)

William H. Harris
(1883-1973)

-dured in the heat of the con - flict: from Christ they in -
-dured_ in the heat of the con - flict: from Christ they in -
-dured_ in the heat of the con - flict: from Christ they in -
them_ in the heat of the con - flict: from

-he - rit a home of un - fad - ing splen - dour,
-he - rit a home_ of un - fad - ing splen - dour, where-
-he - rit a home_ of un - fad - ing splen - dour, un -
Christ they in - he - rit un - fad - - - ing

I heard a voice

Revelation 14: 13

Jeremy Dale Roberts
(b. 1934)

Dedicated to my parents, with love

In My Dreams

Written for The Military Wives Choir,
Jonjo Kerr & Gareth Malone for their first album,
'In My Dreams'

Words & music:
Paul Mealor (b. 1975)

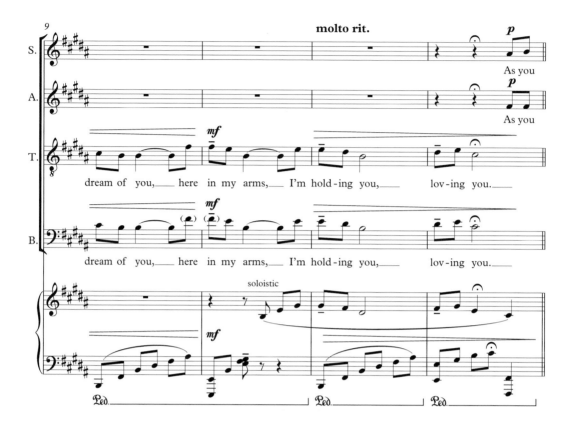

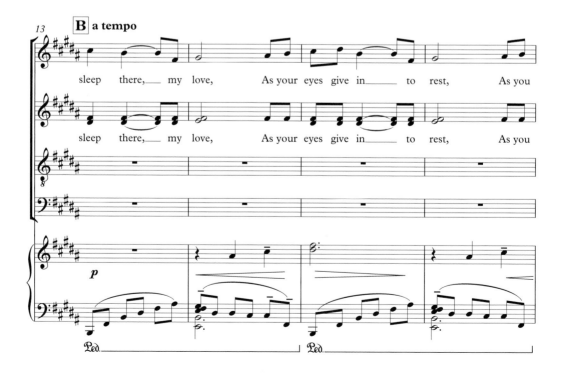

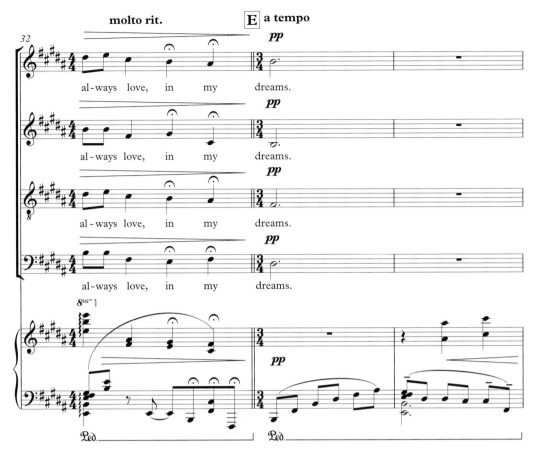

★This section may be sung as a tenor solo

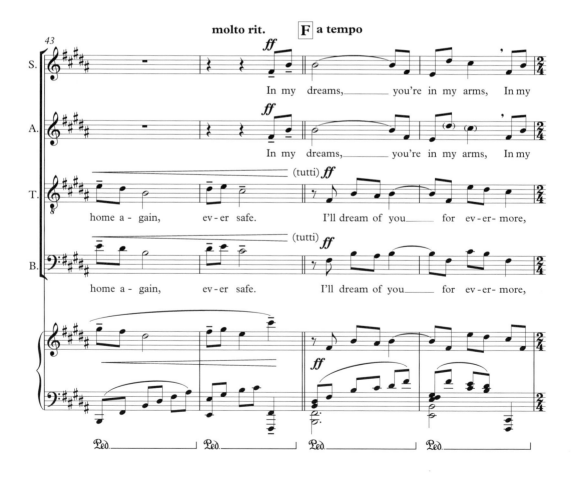

*This section may be sung as a tenor solo

molto rit.

Duration:
3 min. (approx)

Co-commissioned by VocalEssence, Cora Città di Roma, Khorikos and Falu Kammarkör

Nox aurumque

dedicated to Philip Brunelle

Charles Anthony Silvestri
(b. 1965)

Eric Whitacre
(b. 1970)

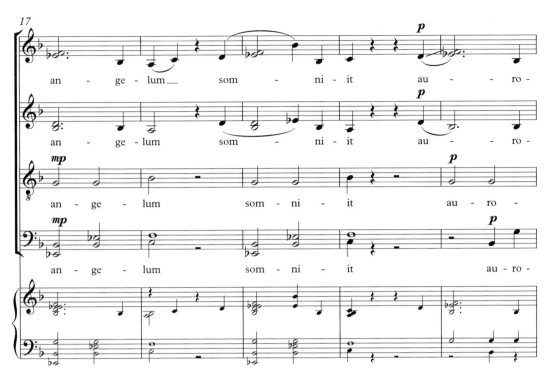

Con moto

In - fu - - - ca - tum tor - pi - dum, au - - - rum,

In - fu - - - ca - tum tor - pi - dum, au - - - rum,

In - fu - sca - tum et au - rum,

In - fu - sca - tum et au - rum,

Poco mosso

Su - sci - - - ta! Su - sci - - -

Su - sci - - - ta!_____ Su - sci - -

Su - sci - ta!_____ Su - sci -

Su - sci - ta! Su - sci -

* elide to sing as 'brex'

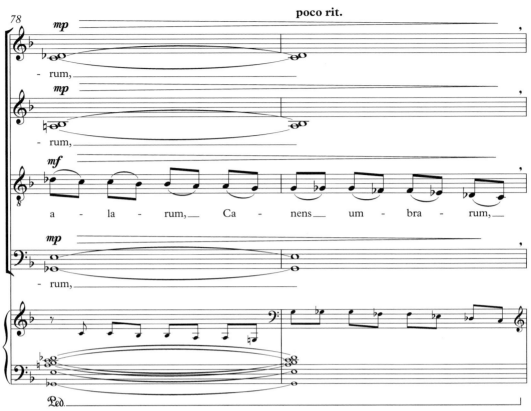

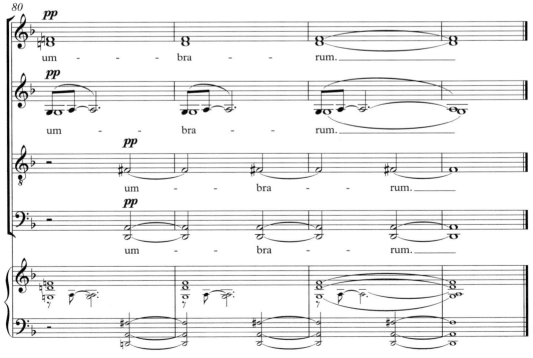

Los Angeles, March 2009

to the memory of John

Requiem aeternam

A choral setting of *Nimrod* from the Enigma Variations.

Text from the
Requiem Mass

Edward Elgar (1857-1934)
arr. David Hill (b. 1957)

* If the top C and B♭ are beyond the range of all the sopranos,
a few, or even one, then the organist should play them instead.

They are at rest

The ver-ses of that hymn which Ser - - aphs chant____
lawn and grove The ver - ses of that hymn which Ser - aphs chant____
lawn and grove The ver - ses of that hymn which Ser - aphs chant____
grove The ver - ses of that hymn which Ser - aphs chant____

Più lento   rit.

____ a - bove. They are at rest,____ they are at rest.
____ a - bove. They are at rest,____ they are at rest.
____ a - bove. They are at rest,____ they are at rest.
____ a - bove. They are at rest,____ they are at rest.

We Remember Them

from *Triptych*

Roland B. Gittelsohn
(1910-1995)

Tarik O'Regan
(b. 1978)

blow - ing of the wind and in the chill of win - ter,_____

we_____

we_____

In the o - pen - ing

re - mem - ber them._____

re - mem - ber them._____

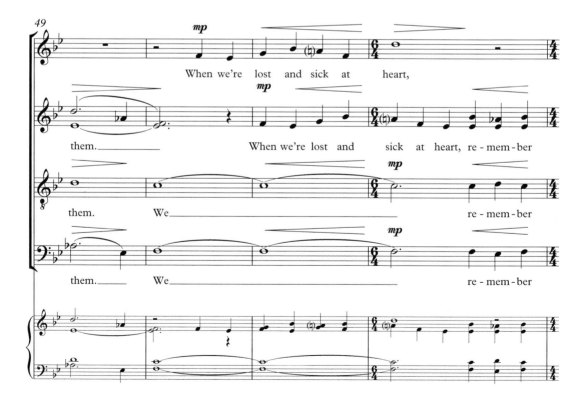

Manhattan, October 2005

We will remember them

Laurence Binyon
(1869-1943)

Edward Elgar (1857-1934)
ed. Ian Tracey (b. 1955)